simple

wire & metal

style

simple

wire & metal

✦ style ✦

DEBORAH SCHNEEBELI MORRELL

Photographs by Heini Schneebeli

Acknowledgements

Very special thanks to Heini Schneebeli for his care and attention to detail in taking the
photographs in this book. My gratitude extends to all the unknown artists and artisans
whose work constantly serves as an inspiration to me.

For my Godchildren
Louis Arthur Lloyd Pack
and
Beatrice Antonia Minns

Published by MQ Publications Ltd.
254-258 Goswell Road, London EC1V 7EB

Copyright © MQ Publications Ltd. 1998

Projects and text © Deborah Schneebeli Morrell 1998

Series Editor: Ljiljana Ortolja-Baird
Editor: Simona Hill
Designer: Bet Ayer
Photographer: Heini Schneebeli

A CIP catalogue record for this book is available from the British Library

ISBN: 1 897954 20 4

1 3 5 7 9 10 8 6 4 2

Printed in Italy

contents

✤

introduction

❖

Metal and wire-work are currently enjoying a resurgence of interest. For those keen to have a go, working with metal and wire is not difficult or beyond the normal range of craft skills. In my attempt to demystify these crafts and to make them accessible to more people, I have designed a range of creative and unusual projects to either decorate the home or to make as gifts. Each project incorporates simple, traditional skills and a range of materials and tools that are available in your local high streets or garden centres. In fact, many tools are common household objects and the need to spend money on expensive equipment will only arise as you make the transition from beginner to experienced craftsperson. Many projects are small enough to be made in an evening and do not require specialist equipment, time consuming preparation or expensive materials. For me, it is this challenge of designing and creating a beautiful project from something so simple and ordinary as a piece of wire or a square of foil which excites my imagination.

Wire

So many types of wire are available, all with different qualities and degrees of pliablility, and it is this infinite adaptability that has made it so appealing to crafts people and artists for centuries. Jewellers and sculptors in particular have exploited the potential of the medium using techniques such as weaving, welding, knotting, moulding, knitting and sewing.

The technique for wire production goes back almost a thousand years, when it was a laborious and intensive hand process. Long before mechanisation, which arrived in England in the mid-16th century, drawing machines were invented and the metal was drawn through holes in a heavy metal draw plate. The iron used at this time corroded quickly. It wasn't until the 19th century that wire was commercially treated by coating it with tin to prevent rust from occurring.

In this era, Britain and France had thriving wire industries for the manufacture of functional and decorative items, from elegant, intricately woven garden furniture to more humble domestic implements. Many examples of wire-work dating from this time can still be seen today and are appealing to collectors. It was only with the invention and mass-production of cheaper plastic products that the demise of wire-based products began.

INTRODUCTION

Some cultures today, notably in third world countries such as Zimbabwe and Zambia, produce the most extrordinarily inventive sculptures using recycled wire, often faithfully reproducing shapes with amazing proportional accuracy. The Masai are famed for weaving brightly coloured baskets from redundant telephone cables. It is not difficult to see why this versatile medium has appeal for artists and craftspeople. American artist Alexander Calder, creator of simple, striking wire sculptures has proved inspirational and his work was the influence for the Hand Ring Holder project on page 20.

Metal

Like wire-work, the art of working with thin sheet metal has a long history, and some outstanding early examples of the craft still exist today. Trade or shop signs, now made from plastic, were once fashioned in the form of the merchandise sold, a boot or shoe for a shoe maker, and a hat for a milliner.

Metal-work craft traditions were imported to the New World from Europe by craftsmen settlers from the late 16th century onwards. in the 19th century a proliferation of followed. Weathervanes, pierced safes are typical examples of what examples of American folk art. signs still exist on 17th-century

When tin became widely available practical and decorative objects lanterns, candle sconces and pie have now become highly prized Stunning examples of elaborate inn central European buildings today.

▶ 9

Mexico has a long-established most metal-work was devoted to candlesticks and highly decorated

tradition of tin ware. Historically religion in the form of altar pieces, frames for sacred icons. Today,

Mexico remains one of the most successful providers of metal crafts to the interior decor and gift trade in Europe and America. The techniques used are simple – like those employed in the projects in the book – cutting, stamping, piercing, scoring and embossing. Other cultures produce fantastic items using recycled metal – a suitcase from Africa made with woven strips of steel cans or a well-designed jug made from colourfully printed oil cans in India. Aluminium, copper or brass would not have been available to these talented folk artists as it was and still is far too expensive to use. For us, it seems relatively inexpensive and easily obtainable.

The skills and techniques involved in producing a wire or metal project may appear intricate and complicated on first sight, since for most of us these are unfamiliar materials to work with. While it is true that 'practice makes perfect', specialist skills are not required, only the imagination to carry your ideas through. My range of projects is simple enough for a beginner to attempt and allows plenty of scope for adapting as your enthusiasm for these versatile media increases.

working with wire

W ire Is a truly versatile medium. Its appeal for me is in the challenge of creating something sophisticated and stylish and above all useful from a material that is plain and non descript in its manufactured form. Twisted, coiled, plaited, looped, bound and beaded, wire can be manipulated into a myriad of shapes using only the aid of basic everyday tools. Improve its strength by twisting strands together and at the same time, twist in a second colour to add an extra dimension to your project. Like metal foil, wire is pliable and extremely durable. It is available in a huge variety of gauges (thicknesses) and metal types. Each varies in thickness, temper and colour.

Most people are familiar with green plastic-coated gardening wire. It is available in different gauges and the thicker wires are extremely springy, but very easy to manipulate. Its plastic coating makes it particularly suited to out-door use. Galvanised wire is com-monly available in five different gauges. It is made of steel and coat-ed with zinc to prevent it from cor-roding and is suitable for outdoor use. Its sturdy properties make it suitable as a strong base for projects which are used as containers.

Soft copper wire has a pink tinge making it particularly appealing for decorative projects. Tinned cop-per wire is stronger than ordinary copper wire and does not tarnish when handled. Brass picture wire is available in short rolls. It is extremely strong since it is made of a number of strands twisted together.

Wire is widely available, relatively cheap to purchase and available in a huge variety of gauges and metal types. All types of wire are suitable for twisting – a technique which produces a decorative, strong and flexible wire. All wire types are available from specialist outlets, while more common, multi-purpose wires are commonly found in garden centres and hardware shops (see suppliers lists for details).

WORKING WITH WIRE

twisted wire
egg spoon

✤

This simple project is a perfect example of the decorative form of the spoon. Twisted galvanised wire can be formed easily into even and symmetrical shapes because the twisting technique produces tension in the wire, making it unlikely to kink. Using one length of wire, the bowl of the spoon is made from wire manipulated into loops, while the handle is formed into a traditional heart.

These decorative projects have a practical function too – you really will be able to toast a piece of bread at an open fire and lift an egg safely out of a pan of boiling water.

Detail of the looped wire manipulated into the bowl of the spoon.

Detail of the twisted wire fork.

p l a n t
s u p p o r t
✤

Antique examples of twisted wire planters and furniture are much sought after. The method of constructing these frames has barely changed. Nowadays, with the development of plastic coated wire, plant structures are longer lasting and are not subject to rust – an advantage if you enjoy working without gloves.

It would be impossible to buy such a pretty and practical plant support for the small cost of making it yourself. These frames are quickly and simply made from twisted thick green garden wire. The technique of twisting adds strength and flexibility. Once you have mastered the technique, the next step is to design your own.

The plant support is sturdy
enough to support most plants.

aluminium mesh basket

❖

Stretched, tucked, pleated or moulded, aluminium mesh is extremely soft, pliable and easy to work with. Obtained from a sculptor's suppliers, it is surprisingly similar to working with fabric, but without the inconvenience of fraying!

The body of the basket is moulded over an upturned bowl and the excess mesh is pleated into shape. The handle, with scroll decoration, is bound to the basket base with fine wire.

Filled with chocolate eggs or sugared almonds at Easter, the basket makes a stunning little gift.

This decorative basket is an example of just how fine wire and mesh can be made to appear.

hand ring
holder

✥

Soft aluminium wire is satisfyingly pliable and although it is relatively thick, it is easy to bend into smooth curves. Contemporary in appearance, this is an easy choice for a beginner, since the techniques required are minimal. The challenge is in manipulating the shape from just one continuous length of wire. The form of the hand is a logical choice for a ring holder, but also ideal for hanging earrings from or draping necklaces over.

A simple template is provided, but as your confidence grows and you become adept at working with wire, design and create your own shapes, such as the bird pictured on page 23.

Once you've mastered the ring hand, design and make your own shapes.

21

beaded
candle holder

❖

Take wire-work techniques one stage further and add a selection of your favourite or most unusual glass beads to create this exquisite candle holder. The wire frame is moulded into the base of a tiny metal tartlet tin, the fluted sides holding the wire evenly in place. The whole of the design and construction of the piece is influenced by the shape and form of the tart case. The basic shape can be adapted to a more complex version once you've mastered the basic techniques.

When lit, the candle flame reflects in each facet of the coloured glass beads, casting a subdued glittering light around the room.

 25

folk art
egg basket
✤

This robust little egg basket made from twisted soft copper wire has all the best qualities of folk art. Although the design is decorative, the pretty looped base acts as a practical stand to raise the basket from the ground making it easier to sit eggs in. The heart motif provides a perfect way to join two ends together. Apart from the base, all the wire used has been twisted, which gives it a decorative charm and makes it stronger so it will keeps its shape better. It is not complicated to make and, as with many of the other projects, requires only the use of wire cutters and pliers. The looped rim and base are made by wrapping the wire around a wooden spoon handle. Once you have made this project try adapting the technique to make other baskets in different shapes and sizes.

26 ◀

picture
frame

❖

A pair of pliers and some wire cutters are the only
tools necessary to create this modern decorated
frame. Aluminium and tinned copper wire are soft, so
can be twisted easily into looped circles. A number of
irregularly-shaped pretty blue and green glass beads
have been threaded onto the silvery wire to offset the
deep blue of the painted round frame. The design
lends itself to displaying a small mirror.

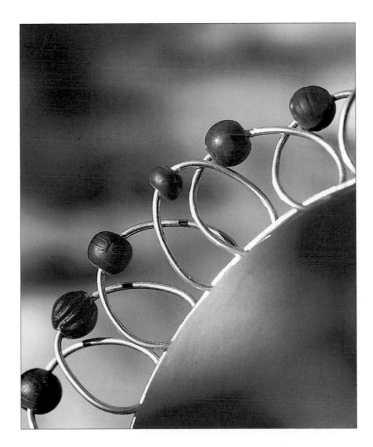

Alternate blue and green glass
beads for best effect.

glass jar
lantern

✣

Find yourself a selection of attractively-shaped glass jars to make into night-light holders. This is one of the simplest projects in the book, requiring few tools and materials or knowledge of complicated techniques. The galvanised wire is twisted tightly onto the rim of the jar, holding the handle securely in place.

Traditional outward-turned scrolls have been used to make the decorative join at the handle tops.

The lanterns have been designed for outside use and look effective arranged in a group or suspended from the branches of a tree.

Detail of the reversed heart-shape scrolls at the handle top.

christmas tree
decorations

❖

These simple candy-striped Christmas tree decorations incorporate wire-work skills on a small scale. Create the candy stripe by twisting in a strand of pink anodised aluminium wire – discarded telephone or electrical wire are good alternatives.

The wire is bent into scrolls, a common decorative feature in wire-work and bound together to form elegant pendant shapes. Iridescent glass beads are suspended from the ornament top.

P

unctured, embossed, folded, snipped, curled and indented – metal foil in all its forms is a versatile, durable and strong medium to work with. Brass, copper and aluminium each have their own unique properties and qualities. While some metal foils lend themselves to different projects, much depends on your personal preference. All are decorated in exactly the same way, but the harder, stronger metals require more pressure to make an impression. Brass is the hardest metal and recognisable for its gold colouring. Copper has a warm pink tinge. It is soft, pliable and easy to cut and decorate. Varnish any copper projects if you do not want the colour to tarnish with age. Aluminium is a soft silvery-white metal, light in weight and very malleable. It will not corrode or tarnish. Metal foils and expanded mesh or woven metal gauze are obtainable in rolls 15cm/6in wide and 1m/1yd long, although some suppliers will cut to your required length. All are readily available from good builder's merchants and specialist craft shops.

The metal foil most commonly used for the projects in this book is 0.1mm, although it is possible to make some projects in other gauges. All the foils are easy to cut with ordinary scissors, although care should always be taken. You will find working with metal foils most rewarding. The results are impressive and professional-looking and people find it hard to believe that they have been made by hand.

cat face
bird scarer

✤

These prowling cats with their striking eyes are just the thing to scare away scavenging birds from the vegetable patch. Any gardener will tell you that pigeons in particular can be real pests pecking away at the brassicas in spring.

   The eyes are made by fixing marbles into holes cut into the foil face. On bright sunny days they become almost luminous when the light shines through them. The effect is eerily realistic.

   Use them decoratively by slotting the wire 'stems' into the top of a garden cane and pushing the cane firmly into the soil.

metal foil
flowers

❖

Most people would never think of making flowers from metal but in reality, they are no more difficult to make than the paper version. The results are unusual, striking and enduring. These flowers were inspired by the ornate flowery metal candlesticks found in French churches. Extend the project and wire the flowers around a candlestick if you are feeling creative.

A tracing wheel has been used to create the pattern. The three-dimensional effect on the petals of the flower was accomplished by marking the lines alternately on the back and front of the cut-out flower.

A combination of all three metal foils has been used for this project – a good opportunity to learn of their different qualities first hand.

▶ 41

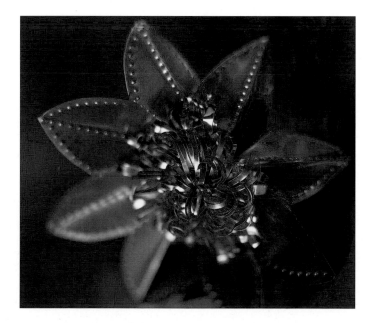

Foil flower with stamen-effect
centres made of copper,
aluminium and brass.

brass
butterfly

✤

Reminiscent of summer's colours with their delicate and intricate markings, these shimmering golden insects will liven up the potting shed wall this winter.

Working with a design which has a symmetrical shape is always satisfying and, since the butterfly shape is decorative, the pattern used for the wing decoration can be less complicated. The three-dimensional effect is made by bending and moulding the body around a wooden spoon handle. For the finishing touch, the antennae are wound around a thin knitting needle to create the tight curls.

The unusual curved 3-dimensional body of the butterfly is made by bending the foil over a wooden spoon handle.

house
candle shade

❖

This unusual candle shade is made from soft aluminium foil but it could be made from thicker aluminium. The design is inspired by Mexican punched tin light or lantern shades. The originals are well-known examples of Mexican tinwork, which is much admired. Tin is more difficult to cut and the edges need to be filed to remove dangerous rough edges.

The tracing wheel lines have punctured the metal allowing the candle light to shine through the tiny holes. The house is illuminated by two night lights placed in glass jars for safety and thick, translucent tracing paper is fixed to the inside walls of the house to obscure the jars.

▶ 45

Disguise bare candle flames with these unusual shades. Holes punctured in the surface of the foil allows the light to shine through.

crown
hook rack

❖

Simple shapes and symmetrical patterns always work well together. This project with its regal theme combines the most traditional wire and metal-work techniques. The embossed metal surface has been decorated using a tracing wheel. The wire-work base is formed from thin twisted copper wire manipulated into the framework, and the hooks and infill detail are made using flattened coils and twisted wire.

For safety, hang below eye level and twist the hooks into an open circle to prevent catching clothes. Its use can be adapted to suit any room in the home – and would be particularly effective nailed inside near the front door as a rack for hanging keys on.

▶ 49

Detail of the embossed surface
of the foil crown.

brass gloved
hand clasp

❖

Based on a common Victorian design, these elegant gloved hands are immensely decorative and useful. The brass is decorated using a tracing wheel and a dry ball-point pen. Brass is a harder metal than aluminium or copper and so needs to be pressed harder to make the pattern clear. Its lovely glowing colour is similar to gold and polishes beautifully using a specialist metal polish.

The clasp part of the design is made by gluing a clothes peg onto the back of the hand using rapid-setting resin glue. Use these glove clasps to hold all manner of things from stamps to decorative ribbons.

Detail of the raised decoration
on the hand of the glove.

b i r d
g r e e t i n g
c a r d

❖

Stamped or embossed metal greeting cards are becoming widely available.

Copper foil is a warm-coloured metal, soft enough to cut with scissors and easy to decorate by drawing and punching a design onto the back to produce a raised pattern on the front. The enduring quality of the metal means that the motif can be removed from the card and used for another decorative purpose, perhaps on the cover of a book, painted box or nailed to a cupboard door.

52 ◀

cheese
larder

❖

You don't need to search far in antique or junk shops to find an inexpensive old food cupboard which will lend itself to converting into a cheese larder. In the past, perforated zinc was commonly used as a screening mesh to keep out flies while American pie safes were traditionally made using punched tin.

Brass gauze is beautiful in combination with the warm gold-effect of the brass foil decoration and complements the pale green cupboard frame. The embossed brass flowers and leaves and the plaited brass wire stems are sewn onto the mesh using fine matching brass wire threaded through the fixing points. These are punched out using a hole punch.

▶ 55

Detail of the hole-punched fixing points on the flowers and leaves.

christmas
reindeer

✤

It takes minimal skill, tools and techniques to make this magical herd of sturdy Christmas reindeer. A backdrop of forest trees made from slightly thicker aluminium foil sets a wintry theme.

The instructions describe a simple system for making a 3-dimensional object from a flat template. The raised pattern which catches and reflects the shimmering light is made by drawing on the back of the soft aluminium foil with a ball-point pen.

This charming collection looks stunning on a Christmas mantelpiece or arranged under a simply-decorated tree. Make them into a mobile by piercing the middle of the top of the back and threading them onto a 1.25mm galvanised or aluminium wire frame.

WORKING WITH METAL

f o i l
w r e a t h

❖

The soft yielding qualities of aluminium foil along with its silvery brilliance make it an ideal material to use to create this unusual wintry wreath. The 'willow leaves' are cut freehand from the metal foil with a pair of scissors and the patterned leaf veins are surprisingly easily drawn using a dressmaker's tracing wheel. Although a little patience is required to fix the finished leaves to the wire frame, the end result of this simple project is quite stunning. The garland could be the focal point in a pale and minimally-decorated room. At a more festive time make it part of a restrained silver and white themed Christmas, perhaps setting the scene by displaying it on your front door.

Detail of the two different willow leaves.

plant name
marker

✤

For those of us who plant a flower only to be unable to identify it months or years later because we've lost the name tag, these unusual plant markers are the perfect solution. The name will never wear away and the tag will not disintegrate.

The key shapes are cut from a roll of thin copper foil and the raised design is created by 'drawing' on the back using a tracing wheel. The decorative stars are punched using a steel punch and a hammer (available from specialist shops). To add a personal touch, use your own handwriting on the front of the marker to name the plant.

Copper is traditionally used for this purpose and its warm colour complements the infinite palette of greens found among foliage in the house or garden. When left outdoors the copper will develop a typical verdigris patination – if you don't want this to happen just give the finished pieces a coat of varnish.

putting it together

▶ 65

materials

❖

1 **Copper foil** (0.1mm thick) – A warm pink metal; soft and very easy to cut and decorate.

2 **Copper strip** (0.2mm thick) – This slightly thicker copper is an alternative that can be used to make the plant name marker on page 63.

3 **Aluminium foil** (0.1mm thick) – A soft and pliable silver metal, easy to cut and decorate.

4 **Brass foil or shim** (0.1mm thick) – A gold-coloured metal; hard and springy, it requires more pressure to decorate.

5 **Aluminium fine expanded mesh** – Extremely soft and pliable. It can be stretched, pleated, tucked, folded or moulded around a solid form as well as cut with scissors.

6 **Woven brass gauze,** eight per centimetre/20 holes per linear inch – Woven gauze is made by weaving together 0.3mm brass wire. It can be manipulated in the same way as aluminium mesh, although it should be cut with strong scissors. Because brass is a relatively hard metal it is not suitable for moulding.

1. **Galvanised wire** – Silver, hard and springy; suitable for outdoor use; available in five different gauges (thicknesses).

2. **Soft copper wire** – Soft and pliable, very easy to use; a warm pink colour which tarnishes with handling and exposure to air.

3. **Brass picture hanging wire** – Sold in small rolls 3m/3yd long at hardware stores; made from a number of strands of wire twisted loosely together; very strong.

4. **Aluminium wire** – Soft and easy to work with.

5. **Tinned copper wire** – Has a shiny finish, does not tarnish; harder than copper wire.

6. **Anodised aluminium wire** – Available in a wonderful array of colours; soft, pliable and easy to work with.

7. **Green gardening wire** – Suitable for outdoor use; easy to manipulate.

8. **Fine wires used for binding** – Available in brass, copper and tinned copper in 0.3mm gauge.

The majority of the tools required for wire and metal work are familiar in many households. The following are commonly found in the household tool chest – wire cutters, pliers, hammer, drill. piece of dowel, and a small piece of wood.

Others will be found around the house – scissors, wooden spoon, knitting needle, ruler, blue tack, transparent and double-sided tape, tracing wheel (more commonly used in sewing), pinking shears, a knitting needle and an old telephone directory.

More specialised equipment includes a hole punch available from good tool shops; a bradawl for puncturing holes in foil and a steel punch with a motif on one end for stamping designs, available from more specialist sculptor's suppliers. A work bench with a vice is useful, quick setting resin glue is necessary for many projects and modelling tools are available from craft suppliers.

essential techniques

✦

Twisting wire

Twisting strands of wire together has many advantages: it looks decorative; it adds strength; and it increases flexibility, making it easier to create smooth spirals and curves.

It is easy to twist strands of soft or fine wire, such as copper, together using a hand-held drill. This method makes it possible to twist wire evenly and as loosely or tightly as the design requires. Harder or thicker wire such as the galvanised or green gardening wire are better twisted by hand using an implement such as a wooden spoon.

Twisting 2mm-thick gardening wire

Cut a length of wire, approximately three times longer than the required twisted length. Bend the wire in half around a fixed point such as a stair banister and join the two ends by twisting them together in an anti-

clockwise direction. Put the handle of a wooden spoon through the loop. Hold the handle in one hand and the spoon section in the other. Twist the wire in a clockwise direction. Pull the wire taut and keep it horizontal for an even twist. When the wire is twisted as tightly as is required, stop turning. Transfer your hold from the spoon to the wire and allow the spoon to unwind slightly and release the tension of the wire. Cut free with wire cutters.

Twisting 1mm soft copper wire

Cut a length of wire approximately half a length longer than the required twisted length. Bend the wire as before, but this time feed the two cut ends into the chuck of a hand drill. Tighten to secure the ends. Keep the wire taut and turn the drill, twisting the wire to the required tension. Undo the chuck to release the wire. Cut the other end from the fixed point.

Gardening wire

Copper wire

Twisting two colours together

Twist soft coloured wire first, as instructed above. Bend thicker wire around the fixed point and twist all thicknesses together around a spoon handle in an anti clockwise direction. Work as for twisting thicker wire.

Twisting two colours together

Making spirals

Curl one end of the wire into a small loop, using pliers. Use your thumb to create an even tension to make a smooth curve.

Making spirals

Judge the distance between the coils by eye

Joining two spirals to make a heart

Bend the straight section of the wire at 45° and bind three times with 1mm galvanised wire. Bind the point where the spirals meet in the same way.

Joining two spirals to make a heart

Plaiting brass picture wire

This is already stranded and twisted. Plaiting makes it thicker and creates an unusual decorative material.

Fix a nail into the work surface. Tie three equal lengths of brass wire together and hook the knot around the nail. Plait evenly until you reach the required length.

Making coils

Plaiting brass picture wire

Making coils

Coils are a useful decorative and structural feature commonly used in traditional wire-work.

Wrap the wire tightly around a wooden spoon handle or dowel, depending on the size of coil required. Thicker wire requires greater manipulation.

Flattening coils

Remove the coil from the wood. Carefully and evenly flatten each loop by pressing each tightly between your fingers. Stretch the coil so that the individual loops are separate or allow them to overlap.

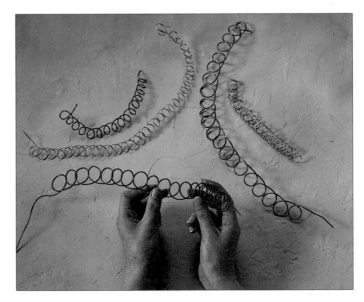

Flattening coils

Embossing aluminium foil

Aluminium is a soft pliable metal, easily marked with a dry ball-point pen. Place the metal onto a yielding surface such as a telephone directory and 'draw' the design by pressing very firmly. Drawing lines against a straight edge produces a quilted effect which appears as a raised surface on the other side.

Copper punching

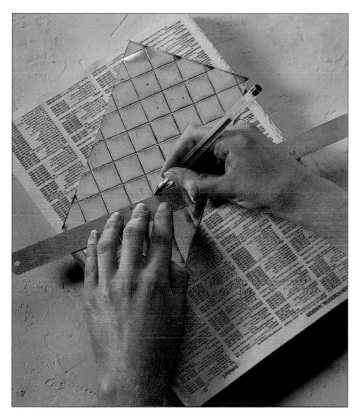

Embossing aluminium foil

Copper punching

Use a ready made punch (available from sculptor's supplier or good tool shops). Punch from the front to create an indented image. Punch from the back and the image will be a raised design on the right side. Place foil on a piece of wood. Position the patterned end of the punch and hit once firmly with a hammer.

Decorating brass using a tracing wheel

Place the metal on a telephone directory. Using the tracing wheel, press firmly to 'draw' directly onto the metal. This is a quick and satisfying method of decorating metal foil – the pattern appears as a series of raised dots on the other side.

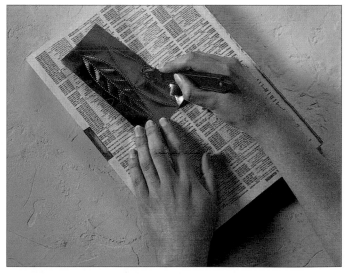

Decorating brass using a tracing wheel

twisted wire egg spoon

✣

Not just a decorative ornament, this twisted wire spoon is practical too!

MATERIALS
◆ *1.25mm-thick twisted galvanised wire – 1.5m/1²⁄₃yd*
◆ *0.75mm-thick galvanised wire – 10cm/4in*
◆ *Wire cutters*
◆ *Bent-nose pliers*

1 Beginning 40cm/15¾in from one end of the wire, make a series of six loops using approximately 30cm/12in in total.

2 Bring together the ends of the looped section to form a circle with the loops facing inwards. Hold the ends together with pliers and make four twists with your free hand.

3 Open the shaft of the handle and form an ellipse 14cm/5in long.

4 Bring the two wires together as before and make four more twists.

5 With pliers, form each wire end into a loose spiral using the same length of wire for each. Join them together so that the spirals touch at one side to make a symmetrical heart.

6 Bind the join four times with the second length of wire and twist the ends tightly together to secure. Trim the excess with wire cutters and tuck the ends out of the way.

plant support

❖

This sturdy plant support is attractive enough to be on display – at least until the plant outgrows it!

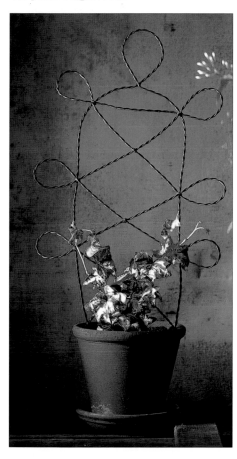

MATERIALS
- ◆ *2mm-thick twisted green gardening wire*
- ◆ *1mm-thick green gardening wire*
- ◆ *Ruler*
- ◆ *Wire cutters*
- ◆ *Bent-nose pliers*

1 Cut a length of twisted wire 1.5m/ 1⅔yd long. Bend the wire loosely in half and form a loop in the middle.

2 Bind the join three times with 1mm-thick wire to secure.

3 Cut a second length of twisted wire 3m/3¼yd long. Bend loosely in half. Form two loops in the second wire 15cm/6in apart. Place the second wire near the top of the first wire and bind the two wires together.

4 Bring the two ends of the long wire across each other. Bind the point where they cross. Make two more loops opposite each other 13cm/5in down the sides of the parallel base wire, binding it together with thin wire as you work.

▶ 73

5 Continue crossing the wire, making loops and binding the wires together until there are three loops on each side. Cross the ends one last time at the centre and bind to hold. Twist the excess wire around the parallel base wire.

aluminium mesh basket

✣

This tiny mesh basket is moulded over a small bowl – the mesh is pleated and tucked into place and held in position with decorative wire-work.

MATERIALS
- *Fine expanded aluminium mesh – 25 x 30cm/9 x 10in*
- *Bowl to use as a mould – 13 x 9 x 6cm deep/5 x 3½ x 2¼in*
- *Scissors*
- *Flat-ended modelling tool*
- *1.25mm-thick, twisted galvanised wire – approximately 3m/3yd*
- *0.75mm-thick, twisted galvanised wire – approximately 3m/3yd*
- *0.3mm-thick, tinned copper wire*
- *Round-nose pliers*
- *Wire cutters*
- *Wooden spoon*

1 Cut one piece of aluminium mesh 23 x 25cm/9 x 10in. Centre the bowl on the mesh. Mould the mesh to fit the outside of the bowl. Make six small tucks at each end to ensure a neat fit. Press firmly to hold the shape.

2 Carefully and evenly cut away the excess mesh from the rim of the bowl.

3 Remove the bowl from the mesh form.

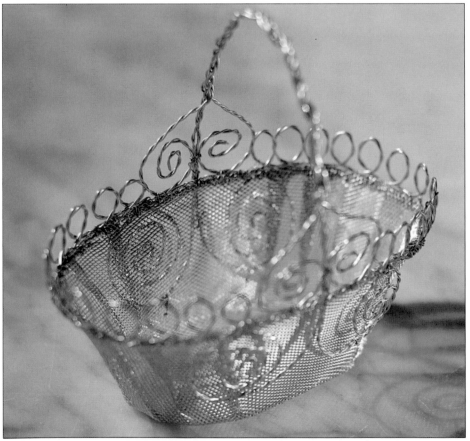

4 To strengthen the basket shape, cut a length of 1.25mm twisted wire to fit exactly the top of the mesh form. Hold it in place and roll the top of the mesh over the wire. Push under with the modelling tool to secure.

5 For the handle, from 0.75mm wire, cut two lengths each 70cm/27½in and two lengths each 45cm/17¾in. Using pliers, form a loose spiral at each end of each wire, with the spiral facing in the same direction.

6 Twist the straight section of the long lengths together to form the handle. Turn the spirals outwards.

7 Bend back the neck of the spiral on the shorter lengths. Twist the shorter lengths one at a time onto the handle, turning the spirals inwards.

8 Position the handle over the side of the basket. Tack on the spirals through the mesh using short lengths of tinned copper wire twisted tightly together. Secure the middle and each side of the spirals as well as the point at which the handle crosses the rim. Add sufficient tacks to make the wire lie flat.

9 Secure the small spirals along the rim of the basket using tinned copper wire. Bind the spirals to the straight part of the handle, forming them into an upside-down heart.

10 Using the 0.75mm twisted wire make a coil over the handle of a wooden spoon (see page 70). Flatten each loop and cut two lengths approximately 13cm/5in to fit along the basket rim at each side of the handle.

11 Bind the loop borders in place using tinned copper wire.

hand ring holder

✤

When twisting the wires together, to protect the surface of the aluminium, put a small piece of paper between the wire and the pliers.

MATERIALS
- ◆ 3mm-thick aluminium wire – 3m/ 3¹/₄yd
- ◆ Template
- ◆ Wire cutters
- ◆ Bent-nose pliers

1 Place the end of the wire over the hand template. Leaving a 10cm/4in end of wire at the base of the palm, carefully bend the wire around the thumb and fingers.

2 Continue bending the wire around the hand and when you come to the wrist make a right-angle turn.

3 Twist the 10cm/4in length of wire very tightly, three times around the remaining longer section of wire using pliers. Trim the excess from the short length only, at the back of the hand.

4 Bind the remaining longer wire length into a tight flat coil forming smooth curves with your thumb and forefinger. (see picture next column)

5 Bind the coil eleven times. Trim the excess at the back of the hand.

6 Pull the coil so that it opens slightly and stands upright – the tighter coils are more difficult to manipulate.

76 ◄

beaded candle holder

✣

Select your favourite or most unusual colourful glass beads for this attractive candle holder.

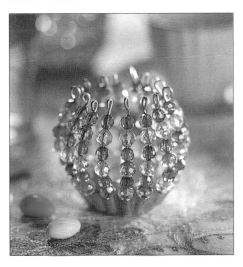

MATERIALS
◆ *1.5mm-thick tinned copper wire*
◆ *Tin tartlet case – 7cm/2¾in diameter*
◆ *Resin glue*
◆ *Spatula*
◆ *Faceted glass beads: shades of pink, red, purple and blue*
◆ *Bent-nose pliers*
◆ *Wire cutters*
◆ *Two hammers*
◆ *Blue tack*

1 Cut eight lengths of wire 26cm/10½in long.

2 Place each wire over a solid metal base and flatten approximately 4cm/1¾in in the middle by hitting hard with the flat side of the head of a hammer.

3 Using the pliers, bend each side of the flattened centre up.

4 Place each wire into the base of the case, overlaying the wires and pushing each side into opposite grooves on the

case sides. Hold the wires temporarily in place with a small piece of blue tack.

5 When all the wires are positioned mix up a quantity of the resin glue and coat the base and the wires with it. Allow it to set before removing the blue tack.

6 Using wire cutters, trim the excess wire.

7 Thread six beads onto each wire, then use the pliers to form a small loop in the top of each wire.

8 With your hands, curve the individual wires into a tulip shape.

folk art egg basket

An ambitious project for those who really enjoy the decorative qualities of traditional wire-work.

MATERIALS
- *Twisted copper wire made with 1.5mm wire*
- *Twisted copper wire made with 1mm wire*
- *Flattened loops made with 1.5mm copper wire*
- *Flattened loops made with 1mm twisted copper wire*
- *A small roll 0.3mm-thick copper binding wire*
- *1mm-thick copper wire*
- *Wire cutters*
- *Bent-nose pliers*

1 Cut two pieces of 1.5mm twisted wire one x 43cm/17in and one x 65cm/25½in.

2 Form an oval with the short length and temporarily bind the two ends together with 1mm-thick wire.

3 Form the second length into a similar oval. Turn back each end at a 45° angle.

4 Using pliers form the ends into inward facing spirals.

5 Push the spirals together to form a heart and bind tightly together with 1mm wire where the spirals touch and again at the base of the heart.

6 Bend the heart up so it sits at right angles to the oval.
(see picture next column)

7 Cut two lengths of 1mm-thick wire each 30cm/12in long. Attach one end of each wire to each side of the heart by twisting the wire end twice around the twisted wire of the oval.

8 Twist the wire around the second oval 6.5cm/2½in away. Continue the wire under the base and up the opposite side, twisting around the ovals as you come to them. The oval with the heart shape will be suspended 6.5cm/2½in above the plain oval.

9 Cut two lengths of 1mm wire each 45cm/17¾in. Form one end of each into a small spiral. Attach each spiral facing inwards, at the base of the heart. Continue to weave each wire around the oval frame, finishing at the top of the opposite side. Trim any excess wire.

10 Cut two lengths of 1mm-thick twisted wire, each 45cm/17¾in long. Weave these wires across the oval frame, working at a right angle to the previous holding wires.

11 Cut one length of 1mm-thick twisted wire, 50cm/19¾in long. Weave this length around the walls of the basket. Twist neatly around one of the upright wires to finish.

12 Cut a 35cm/13¾in length of flattened twisted coils made from the thinner wire. Beginning at the side of the heart, bind the loops onto the top rim using fine wire.

▶ 79

13 Cut a 45cm/17¾in length of the larger coils made with untwisted wire and bind them around the base using fine wire. As you reach the join on the base oval, remove the temporary binding and replace it with finer wire. Trim the excess coils at the point of overlap.

picture frame

✤

Wire is an extremely versatile material. It is readily available in many different metals and can be easily worked without the use of sophisticated techniques or specialised tools. A pair of pliers and some wire cutters are the only tools necessary to create this charming and unusually-decorated frame which makes use of the pliable qualities of aluminium or tinned copper wire. The fact that it is so soft means it can easily be twisted into the looped circle.

1 Using the wire cutters, cut a length of the wire 2m/2yd long. Take care not to bend or twist it at this stage. Thread the beads onto the straight wire.

2 Keeping all the beads to the right side, start to make small loops from the left by bending the wire carefully using about 6cm/2¼in for each loop. Push a single bead into place after the first loop before making the second.

3 Continue making loops and threading the beads until you have enough to stretch around the frame. Now cut another length of wire 80cm/31½in long and thread through the loops until it makes a complete circle with an equal length of wire sticking out at each end.

4 Fit the beaded loops around the edge of the frame, pull the wire tight as shown and twist the two ends together first with your fingers.

5 Twist the two ends firmly together with pliers to make a snug fit around the frame.

6 Turn to the back of the frame and open out the two lengths of wire. Twist the ends with the pliers to make the frame stand.

7 Working from the front of the frame put a dab of glue onto each end of the looped wire, place a bead onto one of the glued ends and push the other end into the bead to make an invisible join.

glass jar lantern

❖

Everyday materials like jam jars look really stunning decorated with twisted wire and with a flickering candle inside, suspended from the bough of a tree.

82 ◄

MATERIALS
- *1mm-thick galvanised wire – one roll*
- *1.25mm-thick galvanised wire – one roll*
- *Wire cutters*
- *Bent-nose pliers*
- *Jam jar*
- *Hand drill*
- *Vice*
- *Small sponge*

1 Cut two lengths of 1.25mm wire, each 1.25m/1⅓yd long.

2 Cut the sponge in half and place one piece at opposite sides of the jam jar to protect the glass. Place the jam jar and sponges in the vice.

3 Place the wire around the rim of the jar and twist clockwise to hold in place.

4 Feed the ends of the wire into the chuck of the drill. Tighten to secure, then wind the drill to twist the wire to the required tension. Pull the wire to keep it taut and hold it horizontal.

5 Release the wire from the chuck, then trim the ends.

6 Turn the jar 180° in the vice, then twist the second length of wire onto the rim in the same way. Trim the wires to the same length.

7 Use the pliers to bend the wire ends into outward facing spirals, pulling the wire against your thumb to produce a smooth curve.

8 Bind the spirals together three times with the 1mm wire. Twist at the back and trim the excess.

christmas tree decorations

✥

Twist a second colour wire into the structure of the scrolls and complement the colour scheme with an attractive glass bead.

MATERIALS
◆ *1.25mm-thick galvanised wire – one roll*
◆ *0.5mm-thick pink anodised alumini-um wire – a small reel*
◆ *Wire cutters*
◆ *Bent-nose pliers*
◆ *Glass beads – two small iridescent, one red heart, two pink cut-glass*
◆ *Small scissors*

1 Twist together the two lengths of wire following the instructions on page 69.

2 Using wire cutters, cut four lengths of twisted wire each 22cm/8¾in.

3 Form one end of each length into a large loose spiral. Make a curve in the central section, then form a tight spiral at the other end. Make four.

4 Cut one length of pink wire 22cm/8¾in. Thread a small iridescent bead half way along. Bend the wire in two around the bead, then thread the remaining beads onto both wires.

5 Put the four scrolls together, with the bend facing outwards. Place the beaded wire in the centre of the large scroll. Tightly bind the top join approximately eight times with pink wire.

▶ 83

6 Twist the ends together to secure. Bind the base in the same manner.

7 Open out the shape, ensuring that the scrolls are evenly spaced.

cat face bird scarer

On a light spring or summer's day, these decorative cats will be sure to scare away the birds.

MATERIALS
◆ 0.15mm-thick copper foil – 30cm/12in square
◆ 2mm-thick copper wire – one roll
◆ Tracing paper, pencil and glue
◆ Thin card
◆ Dry ball-point pen
◆ Small coin
◆ Small-pointed scissors
◆ Tracing wheel
◆ Old telephone directory
◆ Resin glue and spatula
◆ Transparent tape
◆ Two glass marbles
◆ Bent-nose pliers
◆ Bamboo cane

1 To make a template, trace or photocopy the pattern provided. Stick the copy to thin card and cut out. Tape the template to the copper foil.

2 Draw the outline with a ball-point pen, pressing lightly to transfer the shape onto the metal.

3 Cut out the face and remove the circles marked for the eyes. Using the points of the scissors, snip all around the edges of the eyes, to make sure that the marbles will fit neatly.

5 Mark the whiskers with the tracing wheel.

7 Cut a 30cm/12in length of copper wire. Use the pliers to make a double loop at one end, ensuring that the two loops are firmly closed together.

4 Place the face on the directory. With the tracing wheel, outline the face, circle the eyes and outline the ears. Use the ball-point pen to draw in the nose, mouth and the effect of fur in the ears and over the top of the face. Press firmly to make sure the design is clearly marked.

6 Turn over to the right side of the face. Mix up the resin glue and apply all around the perimeter of the eyes. Place each marble in the eye, over the glue and allow to dry. Support the underside of the face so that the marbles do not become dislodged.

8 Make a mix of resin glue and slide the base of the face between the loops. Fill the space inside the loop with glue making sure that both the wire and metal are covered.

▶ 85

metal foil flowers

Use all three metals – copper, aluminium and brass – to make these delicate flowers.

MATERIALS
- 0.1mm brass foil or shim – one roll
- 0.1mm-thick scraps of copper and aluminium foil – 3 x 10cm/1¼ x 4in
- 1mm- and 1.5mm-thick copper wire – approximately 30cm/12in per flower
- Tracing paper and pencil
- Thin card and glue
- Dry ball-point pen
- Transparent tape
- Old telephone directory
- Tracing wheel
- Small-pointed scissors
- Medium-size scissors
- Bradawl
- Resin glue
- Spatula
- Pliers

1 To make a template, trace or photocopy the pattern provided. Stick the copy to thin card and cut out. Tape the template to the brass foil.

2 Draw the outline with a ball-point pen, pressing lightly to transfer the image.

3 Cut out the shape using small scissors. Pierce the centre with the bradawl, insert the point of the scissors and cut out the circle.

4 Place the flower on the directory. Use the tracing wheel to mark the lines between the petals.

5 Turn the flower over and mark the longer lines in the centre of the petals and around the edge of the flower. This method creates a 3-dimensional effect.

6 To make stamens, cut one length each of aluminium, copper and brass foil 3 x 10cm/1¼ x 4in.

7 Snip closely along one side – the snipped edge will curl automatically giving the frilly appearance of a stamen.

8 Cut a 30cm/12in length of 1.5mm wire and make a small loop at one end using pliers.

9 Wind the frilly brass foil tightly around the wire, then add the copper and finally the aluminium.

10 Pinch the frilly edge of foil onto the wire stem using pliers.

11 Thread through the flower centre, push firmly against the petals.

12 Make a mix of glue. Use the spatula to apply glue around the underside of the petals where they meet the stem. Allow to dry.

13 Wind a 30cm/12in length of 1mm-thick copper wire tightly around the stem. Allow the glue to nearly dry.

14 Continue up the stem and wind around the base of the flower head making sure that the untidy join is neatly covered. Snip off the excess wire.

brass butterfly

These 3-dimensional shapes are simple to make. Their bodies are moulded around a wooden spoon handle and their antennae are springy coils of foil.

MATERIALS

◆ *0.1mm-thick brass foil or shim – one roll*
◆ *Tracing paper and pencil*
◆ *Thin card and glue*
◆ *Transparent tape*
◆ *Dry ball-point pen and a small coin*

◆ *Small-pointed scissors*
◆ *Old telephone directory*
◆ *Two sizes of tracing wheel*
◆ *Wooden spoon and knitting needle*
◆ *Brass picture wire*

1 To make a template, trace or photocopy the pattern provided. Stick the copy to card and cut out. Tape the template to the brass foil and draw around the shape pressing lightly with a ball-point pen.

2 Remove the template. Using small-pointed scissors cut out the butterfly, taking care when cutting the antennae. Cut between each pair of wings.

3 Place the butterfly on an old directory. Outline the body and wings with a large tracing wheel. Mark a circle on each wing by drawing around a coin with a dry ball-point pen.

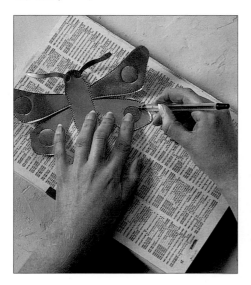

4 Use the smaller tracing wheel to make stars in the circles and lines across the body. Use the larger wheel along each antennae and to make three lines where each wing joins the body.

5 Turn the butterfly to the right side. Bend the wings into position. Curl the body section around the handle of a wooden spoon.

6 To make the antennae, roll each tightly around a knitting needle as shown in the picture below. Remove the needle and loosen the coil.

7 Use resin glue to secure a small brass wire hook to the back of the body. This allows the butterfly to be hung.

house candle shade

Soften lighting with these unusual candle shades, inspired by traditional Mexican crafts. Made in the form of a simple house, these shades look stunning when the light shines through the windows and the punched holes.

MATERIALS

- ◆ 0.1mm-thick aluminium foil
- ◆ Tracing paper, glue
- ◆ Dry ball-point pen
- ◆ Ruler and pencil
- ◆ Craft knife and thin card
- ◆ Two tracing wheels – one with closely-spaced and one with widely-spaced wheels
- ◆ Old telephone directory
- ◆ Small-pointed scissors
- ◆ Transparent tape

1 To make a template, trace or photo-copy the pattern provided. Stick the copy to card and cut out. Tape the template to the aluminium foil. Draw the outlines of the house, windows and door with a ball-point pen, pressing lightly to transfer the shape.

3 Remove the template and cut care-fully around the shape. To cut the windows, first make a cut in each corner with a craft knife, then push the scissors through.

5 Using the larger tracing wheel and a ruler, re-draw the lightly-drawn guide lines. Press very hard so that the points on the wheel pierce through the metal. Use a ruler for drawing the straight lines.

2 Use the ruler and pen to draw lightly over the lines marked on the template – these will appear as indented lines on the metal.

4 Place the foil right side down on the directory. Draw lines around the windows with the small tracing wheel, pressing firmly to transfer the design.

6 With the help of a ruler, bend the roof at a 45° angle. Bend the chimneys upright, then bend each side at right angles to the house front.

▶ 91

crown hook rack

✤

This hook rack, with its regal theme, can be adapted to suit any room of the house.

MATERIALS
- 0.1mm-thick copper foil
- 0.3mm-thick reel of copper wire
- 1mm-thick twisted copper wire – approximately 3m/3yd
- 1.5mm-thick copper wire – one reel
- Tracing paper
- Pencil
- Glue
- Thin card
- Transparent tape
- Old telephone directory
- Small piece of wood
- Small-pointed scissors
- Dry ball-point pen
- Tracing wheel
- Bent-nose pliers
- Long-nose pliers
- Bradawl
- Wire cutters

1 To make a template, trace or photo-copy the pattern provided. Stick the copy to card and cut out.

2 Tape the template to the copper foil. Draw around the outline with a dry ball-point pen pressing lightly to transfer the image.

3 Carefully cut out the shape using small pointed scissors. Snip off the sharp corners.

4 Place the crown on the directory. Outline the crown using the tracing wheel. Draw two parallel lines across the lower part of the design. Divide the section between the lines into three and mark the design in each section. Add a scroll pattern to the top half of the design.

5 To make the loop decoration, cut a length of 1mm-thick twisted copper wire 40cm/15¾in. At one end, fold 2cm/1in up at a right angle. Bend the wire into a rectangular shape to correspond with the section at the base of the crown below the parallel line decoration. Bring it round where it meets. Make another right-angle return of 3cm/1¼in to match the beginning.

6 Cut and manipulate a row of flattened loops so that they fit into the wire shape made at step 4. Use the fine wire to bind the loops in place.

7 Cut 10cm/4in lengths of the twisted wire and use the pliers to bend one end to make them into hooks.

8 Place the crown right side up, over the piece of wood. Use the bradawl to pierce four holes along the base line of the crown – one in the middle of each section and one larger one at the join between the first and second sections. (see picture next column)

9 Push the two ends of the loop decoration through the larger hole. Bend the top 2cm/1in of each hook over at right angles and push these through the designated holes.

10 Turn the crown over. Use the long-nose pliers to bend and flatten any protruding wire ends.

brass gloved hand clasp

✢

These Victorian-style little gloved hands ingeniously disguise a wooden peg clasp. The glowing colour of brass is similar in appearance to gold and polishes beautifully. Use them to hold all types of items from stamps to ribbons.

MATERIALS
- 0.1mm-thick brass foil or shim – one roll
- Tracing paper and pencil
- Thin card and glue
- Transparent tape

- Small-pointed scissors
- Tracing wheel
- Dry ball-point pen.
- Old telephone directory
- Quick-setting resin glue and spatula
- Wooden clothes peg

1 To make a template, trace or photocopy the pattern provided. Stick the copy to card and cut out. Tape the template to the metal foil.

2 Draw around it with a dry ball-point pen to transfer the shape.

3 Cut out carefully, paying attention to the intricate areas around the fingers.

4 Place the glove right side down on the directory and decorate the surface with the tracing wheel, pressing firmly. The design will appear as a raised pattern on the right side. Trace a line all around the edge of the glove and decorate the cuff.

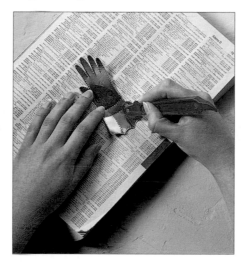

5 With the pen, make dots where the fingers join the hand and along the band around the wrist. Mark the spirals and the star on the back of the hand and the pattern on the cuff.

6 Mix a small quantity of resin glue. Use the spatula to apply it in a straight line along the wrong side of the hand to correspond with the length of the peg.

7 Stick the peg to this glued area, making sure the lever end matches the cuff. Put a weight onto the peg and leave the glue to set.

bird greeting card

These embossed greeting cards are simple to decorate using a tracing wheel and punched stars.

MATERIALS

- ◆ 0.1mm-thick copper foil
- ◆ Tracing paper and pencil
- ◆ Thin card and glue
- ◆ Transparent tape
- ◆ Double-sided tape
- ◆ Old telephone directory
- ◆ Dry ball-point pen
- ◆ Brown card – 16 x 22cm/ 6¼ x 8½in
- ◆ Tracing wheel
- ◆ Blue handmade paper 16 x 9cm/ 6¼ x 3½in
- ◆ Small-pointed scissors
- ◆ Pinking shears
- ◆ Star punch and hammer
- ◆ Small piece of wood

1 To make a template, trace or photocopy the pattern provided. Stick the copy to card and cut out. Tape the template to the copper. Draw the outline with a ball-point pen pressing lightly to transfer the design.

2 Remove the template. Cut out the shape.

3 Place the shape right side down on an old directory. Outline the shape, pressing firmly with the tracing wheel. 'Draw' two parallel lines at the base of the neck, then four lines to separate the tail from the body.
(see picture next column)

4 With the tracing wheel, draw two lines at each side of the wing.

5 Transfer the bird to the wood surface. Using a hammer, punch five stars along the centre of the wing, one for the eye and five along the tip of the tall.

6 Fold the brown greeting card in half so that it stands with the opening at the base.

7 Trim the edge of the blue paper with pinking shears. Apply two strips of double-sided tape to one side.

8 Centre the blue rectangle, then stick in place on the brown card.

9 Centre the bird on the paper and stick in place using the double-sided tape.

10 Press lightly to ensure the bird is secure.

cheese larder

❖

A combination of wire- and metal-work techniques has been used to create this useful and decorative cheese larder.

MATERIALS
- ◆ 0.1mm-thick brass foil – one roll
- ◆ 0.3mm-thick brass wire – one reel
- ◆ Woven brass gauze
- ◆ Plaited brass picture wire – 1m/1yd
- ◆ Tracing paper and pencil
- ◆ Thin card and glue
- ◆ Dry ball-point pen and coin
- ◆ Transparent tape
- ◆ Old telephone directory
- ◆ Small hole punch
- ◆ Tracing wheel
- ◆ Brass drawing pins
- ◆ Hammer
- ◆ Small-scale larder cupboard or MDF blank with the front panel cut away

1 To make a template, trace or photo-copy the pattern provided. Stick the copy to card and cut out.

2 Tape the template to the brass foil and draw around the shape pressing lightly with a ball-point pen.

3 Remove the templates and place the foil onto the directory. Mark the leaf veins and the petals with the tracing wheel.

4 Draw around the coin to make the flower centre. Then make five flowers, six leaves and one flowerpot.

5 With the tracing wheel, draw the pot outline. Draw three circles in the top section and decorate them with tracing wheel stars. Make dots between these with the point of the ball-point pen.

6 Add a lattice-work design to the lower section of the pot.

7 Cut carefully around all the shapes. For safety, cut off the sharp corners of the pot.

8 Using the hole punch, make holes in each end of the leaves, on the tip of alternate flower petals, then three evenly-spaced holes up each side of the pot.

9 Cut a piece of gauze 3cm/1¼in larger all around than the panel in the cupboard door. With a pencil, draw the shape of the panel in the centre of the gauze.

10 Centre the pot 2cm/¾in above the drawn baseline. Secure by tying the fine brass wire through the punched holes and through the gauze. Twist to secure tightly on the wrong side.
(see picture next column)

11 Cut five plaited brass lengths: one x 18cm/7in, two x 14cm/5½in and two x 8cm/3¼in. Slot each wire behind the pot and tie onto the gauze using fine wire. Secure as before.

12 Place one flower on each stem and tie in place.

13 Add two leaves to each of the three central stems.

14 Check that all the ties are secure on the back of the gauze, then trim the excess.

15 Position the gauze over the space on the inside of the cupboard door, ensuring the design is facing in the correct direction. Push a line of brass drawing pins into the frame all around the gauze and hammer in place.

christmas reindeer

✥

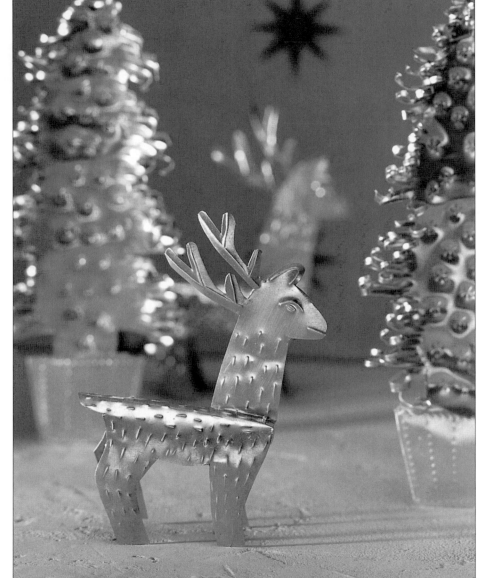

This his magical herd of reindeer make a stunning and unusual Christmas decoration.

MATERIALS
◆ *0.1mm-thick aluminium foil –*
15cm/6in square for each reindeer
◆ *Tracing paper and pencil*
◆ *Thin card and glue*
◆ *Dry ball-point pen*
◆ *Transparent tape*
◆ *Small-pointed scissors*
◆ *Telephone directory*
◆ *Bent-nose pliers*

1 To make a template, trace or photo-copy the pattern provided. Stick the copy to card and cut out.

2 Tape the templates onto the alumini-um foil. Draw around each outline.

3 Remove the templates. Carefully cut out each shape using small-pointed scissors. Take special care with the antlers.

4 Place the shapes on an old directory. Mark the body pattern by pressing with a dry ball-point pen. Mark short lines along the back and then at right angles down the legs. Mark the eye, mouth, antlers and neck.

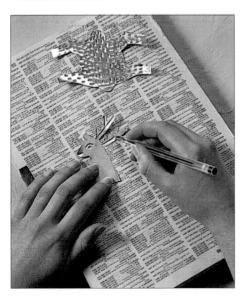

5 Cut a 0.5cm/⅛in slit at each side of the base of the neck, 0.5cm/⅛in up from the base. Turn the cut sections in and press flat.

6 Make a slit in the front of the reindeer body large enough to fit the the base of the neck through. Push the neck through the slit.

7 To secure the head firmly to the body, turn the body to the wrong side and use the pliers to open out the folded-in sections.

8 Bend the tab at the front of the body down, then bend the body over to enable the reindeer to stand.

foil wreath

❖

Silver aluminium is the perfect metal with which to create the subtly-decorated willow leaves which make up this wintry wreath.

MATERIALS
- *0.1mm-thick aluminium foil – one roll*
- *Tracing paper, pencil, thin card and glue*
- *1mm-thick galvanised wire – one roll*
- *Twisted galvanised wire made from 1.5mm wire – 22cm/8½in*
- *0.3mm-thick tinned copper binding wire – one reel*
- *Tracing wheel and bradawl*
- *Small-pointed scissors*
- *Dry ball-point pen*
- *Telephone directory*
- *Small block of wood*
- *Transparent tape*

1 Using twisted wire, form a circle with a 18cm/7in diameter. Bind the join with the 1mm wire.

2 To make a template, trace or photocopy the pattern provided. Stick the copy to card and cut out. Tape the templates to the metal foil and draw around each using a ball-point pen. Draw 50 in total. Remove the templates.

3 Place the foil on the directory. Use the tracing wheel to mark the leaf veins. One leaf has an outline and a central vein. The other has veins radiating from the central vein.

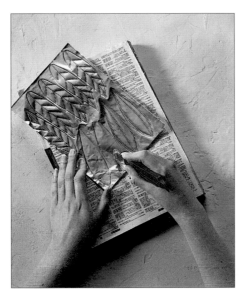

4 Carefully cut out the leaves. Clip off any sharp points.

5 Place each leaf on the wood and push the tip of the bradawl through the base of each leaf to make a very small hole.

6 Thread fine wire through the hole and bind it tightly onto the twisted wire circle. Thread the leaf shapes alternately and space evenly to complete the circle.

7 Add a second layer of leaves overlapping the first, threading each onto the circle as before.

▶ 103

8 Manipulate the leaves with your finger, bending, twisting and curling them slightly to give a more natural appearance.

plant name marker

❖

These copper plant tags are suitable as a first project for a beginner.

MATERIALS

- ◆ 0.1mm-thick copper foil
- ◆ Tracing paper and pencil
- ◆ Thin card and glue
- ◆ Dry ball-point pen
- ◆ Two different-sized tracing wheels
- ◆ Star punch and hammer
- ◆ Small-pointed scissors
- ◆ Transparent tape
- ◆ Old telephone directory
- ◆ Small block of wood

1 To make a template, trace or photo-copy the pattern provided. Stick the copy to card and cut out. Tape the tracing to copper foil and draw around it with the ball-point pen to make an indent. Cut out each shape.

2 Place each shape on an old directory. Draw around the edge with the small tracing wheel, pressing firmly to create the indented dotted line. The pattern will appear as a raised design on the right side of the key.

3 In the same way, roll the larger tracing wheel along the middle of the 'stem' to produce a similar pattern.

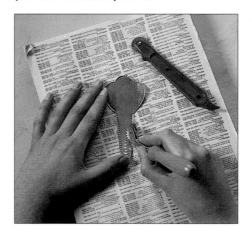

4 Place the plant marker on a piece of wood. Position the star punch at the top, then at the base of the central section. Hit with the hammer to transfer the design.

5 To finish, using the directory for a surface, write the name of the plant in the central section with a dry ball-point pen.

t e m p l a t e s

cat face bird scarer

christmas reindeer
body

christmas reindeer
head

All templates actual size

All templates actual size

brass damselfly

metal foil flowers

106 ◀

bird greeting card

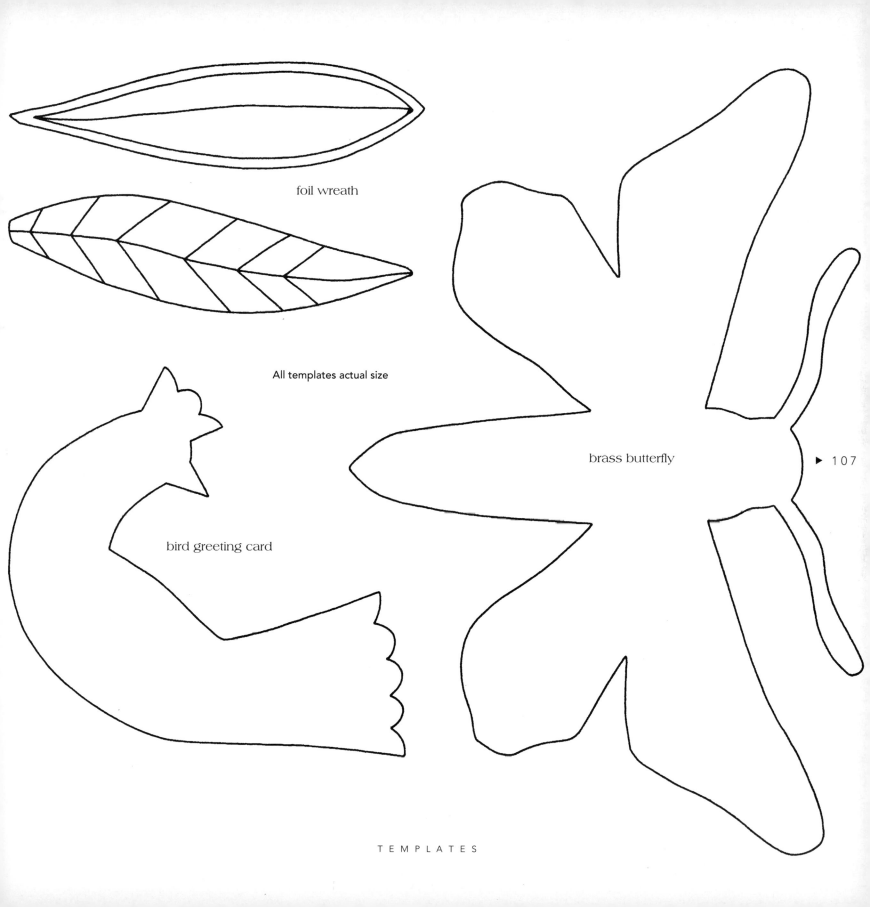

foil wreath

All templates actual size

brass butterfly

▶ 107

bird greeting card

brass gloved
hand clasp

crown hook rack
reverse the image at the broken line

All templates actual size

house candle shade
Join the two halves together
and cut as one piece

All templates
actual size

plant pot for the
cheese larder

leaf for the
cheese larder

flower for the
cheese larder

house candle shade
Join the two halves together
and cut as one piece

plant name marker

ring hand
Actual size

suppliers

❖

ALEC TIRANTI LTD
27 Warren Street
London W1P 5DG
Tel: 0171 636 8565
– suppliers of brass, aluminium, copper
foil and some wires.

J SMITH & SONS
42–56 Tottenham Road
London N1 4BZ
Tel: 0171 253 1277
– non ferrous metal stockholders
– suppliers of brass gauze, metal foils
and wires. Catalogue available.

SCIENTIFIC WIRE COMPANY
18 Raven Road
London E18 1HW
Tel: 0181 505 0002
– specialist and mail order supplier of a
large variety of wire.

In addition most hardware and tool
shops stock a variety of wire. Garden
centres, hardware stores, craft and
jewellery-making shops are all good
sources of material.

▶ 111

index

❖

Numbers in italics indicate photographs